It's About TIME

Why Are People *Late*?

Richard B. Hatcher

HATCHBACK Publishing
Genesee, Michigan

It's About Time - Why Are People Late?
©2019 Richard B. Hatcher

All Rights Reserved. In accordance with the U.S. Copyright Act of 1976, the scanning, uploading, and electronic sharing of any part of this book without the permission of the publisher is unlawful piracy and theft of the author's intellectual property. If you would like to use material from the book (other than for review purposes), we ask you to please cite your reference. Thank you for your support of the author's rights.

HATCHBACK Publishing LLC
Genesee, Michigan 48437
Since 2005

The views, opinions and words expressed in this book are those of the author and does not necessarily reflect the position of HATCHBACK Publishing LLC or its owners.

ISBN 978-1-948708-33-3

Printed in the United States

Content

Introduction…..5

Chapter 1 Statistics and Stories…..7

Chapter 2 Why Are People Late?.....15

Chapter 3 How To Be On Time…..21

Conclusion…..25

Author Bio…..27

Reference List…..31

Introduction

"I'm late, I'm late for a very important date. No time to say hello, goodbye, I'm late, I'm late, I'm late." You may remember this quote from the white rabbit in Disney's *Alice in Wonderland*.

Like Alice tumbling down the rabbit hole, having a conversation with herself, we find ourselves in our own wonderland of excuses and denial when it comes this one question: Why am I always late?

This book seeks to help those of us who struggle with being late more than we would like. A person who is late or behind time is called tardy. The term suggests habitual lateness.

If you describe someone as being tardy, you are criticizing them because they are sluggish to act. When you are late for something you are tardy. Tardiness refers to the habit of being late. A habit is a settled or regular tendency or practice, especially one that is hard to give up.

This book will help you overcome the habit of being late by helping you choose a substitute for your tardiness, cutting out as many triggers as possible and encouraging you to surround yourself with people who live the way you want to live.

You must visualize yourself succeeding. You don't need to become someone else, you just need to return to the old you. Its time to come out of the rabbit hole.

Chapter 1

Statistics and Stories

Because of my upbringing in athletics and the military, statistics have always been important to me. The field of statistics is the science of learning from data.

Contrary to my personal research from Stephn/Flickr of an article dated March 11, 2015, it is unfortunate I found things have gotten progressively worse.

Statistics

Thirty percent of Americans admitted to being late for work at least once per week. The biggest threat to punctuality is traffic, with 49% of respondents claiming this is why they are late. Bad weather is also mentioned as a cause for tardiness by 26% of the respondents. Thirty-two percent of Americans admitted they were late simply because there were no consequences for being late at their place of employment.

Oversleeping was reported by 49% of respondents. Among parents with children, 27% of parents put their jobs at risk in order to meet transportation needs. Forty percent of parent's work schedules are affected because of shuttling children around. Forty three percent claim to be late due to issues of getting their family up and ready for the day. Sixty percent of Americans categorize themselves as disorganized resulting in being late to work or school because of misplaced items. Forty percent of Americans underestimate how long a task will take. While 53% of American employers expect their employees to be on time, 41% fire someone for habitually being late.

When CEOs' are late by ten minutes every day, it costs the US economy 90 billion dollars each year in lost productivity.

We can all admit speeding tickets and accidents (some unfortunately causing death) are results of people running late.

Statistics are interesting and we can

certainly learn from the data collected by them. In the end they still show us the only two reasons people run late are:

1. Emergencies which are unforeseen combination of circumstances that result in an immediate call for action.

2. Excuses which is the attempt to lessen blame and seek to defend or justify our actions.

All of us will experience an emergency from time to time that will cause us to be late, but they should be few and far in-between. If they are not, then we must take a serious look to see if we are headed down the road of the excuse maker. The more we make excuses, the easier it is to make even more excuses. The cure for excuses is proper execution.

Stories

Mt. Vesuvius

The following stories are examples of events that happened in the past which caused tragedies because people were late. Regardless if the event was manmade or nature made, if time had been observed loss of life and property would have been a lot less.

Mt. Vesuvius, on the coast of Italy, is the most active volcano in Europe. It is considered to be one of the most dangerous volcanos in the world because of its proximity to the city of Naples. Mt. Vesuvius destroyed the city of Pompeii, a city south of Rome, in A.D. 79 in twenty-five hours. The major quake was followed by several minor quakes throughout the following years. This was a warning that it was time to move.

Because the earth vibration activity was so common in the area, people paid little attention in early August of A.D. 79 when several quakes shook the city of Pompeii. People were unprepared for the explosion that took place shortly after noon August 24 A.D. Two thousand people survived the first explosion. Instead of heeding the warning of impending doom, the people stayed.

Ash blocked the sun by 1:00p.m. The people tried to clear heavy ash from the rooftops as it fell at a rate of six inches an hour. Shortly after midnight, a wall of volcanic mud swallowed the town of Herculaneum crushing it. Pompeii was not far, only ten miles away and the citizens of Herculaneum fled in that direction.

Around 6:30 a.m. on the following morning, a cloud of volcanic ash rolled down Vesuvius' slopes and covered the city of Pompeii. Most victims died instantly. Their bodies were in a semi-curled position, buried in ash and preserved for hundreds of years. It is believed that 30,000 people died from the eruption of Vesuvius. All that death happened because people did not react in a timely fashion.

Communist Party

It was July 30, 1921 when the police

arrived at a house in the French con session of Shanghai. They were several hours late after the first initial call. Twenty-eight years later, the communist party took the country. The entire group, while having their first meeting, could have been arrested if the police would have arrived on time. Today, China would be a very different country.

The RMS Titanic

More than a century after the Titanic sank, a new theory has been suggested. It was said the radio operator did not pass along the last clearest warning about possible icebergs to Captain Edward Smith in a timely manner.

The reason for the oversight was that the message did not have the prefix "MSG" (Masters Service -Gram), which required a Captain to personally acknowledge that he had received the message. Thus the radio operator deemed the message non-urgent and did not deliver it promptly.

Pearl Harbor

Again seen as a surprise attack that would throw the United States into WW II, the bombing of Pearl Harbor bore plenty of warnings.

Then President, Franklin D. Roosevelt, had been warned by many of his generals that the Japanese would target a surprise attack on Hawaii or Alaska without declaring war. Days before the actual attack Japanese plans were widely spotted doing scouting operations on specific U.S. ports. Three days before Pearl Harbor was attacked, Roosevelt was even handed a telegram that told him the Japanese were planning an attack on U.S. soil.

President Franklin D. Roosevelt, did not act on the information given to him in a timely manner which could have prevented so much damage and loss of life.

Many of us will not see our lateness as a cause for property damage or loss of life. It can and does cause damage to something important…our reputation.

Chapter 2

Why are People Late?

The infamous white rabbit from Alice in Wonderland's mantra was *I'm late, I'm late, for a very important date.* He said this over and over again to himself. His reputation was his identity. He was the late character.

If you think of yourself as the person that is always late guess what, you will always be late. If you have ever said to someone, you are going to be late for your own funeral, or they are on CPT (Colored People Time) you have just helped solidify that persons' internal talk to themselves about being late. People will practice being late to uphold their reputation.

People are late often as an expression of power. There is a concern if someone is constantly late for daily appointments and scheduled assignments. But if they can be on time when the CEO calls for a meeting, they may be saying, "You are less powerful than me, so you have to wait for me. This meeting does not start until I show up."

People are late because they are too optimistic. The optimist thinks the car will always start, I will catch all the green lights, I will not get caught by the train, the weather is holding up, I think I have plenty of gas in the tank. They cut time so short that if the slightest thing goes wrong they are late…again.

People are late because there is no visible reward for being on time. Behavior allowed will increase in frequency. Terror, misery, weariness, and indignation are primary motivating factors in human beings. Unless there is a reward for being on time, other than your reputation or a punishment for not being on time, why not be late?

People are late because they find it difficult to say no. This person often wants to be accepted, belong in the inner circle, or at the proverbial cool peoples' table. They sometimes have self-esteem issues and may have been bullied when they were younger. They are yes people. They will say, "Sure I'll do it," even though it conflicts with their schedule. Unable to say no, they use lateness as a tool in the hopes they won't soon be asked again for another request.

Some people are late because they are drama kings or queens. They love the attention being late brings. When you come into a room late, all eyes are upon you. They have become addicted to the adrenaline rush they get and convince themselves they must be late.

People are late because they are unorganized, lazy, and uncommitted. Whatever the reason, short of a medical condition, there is no excuse for being late. The saying which came from the British army, is still true today: *prior preparation prevents poor performance.* Being late is unprofessional. It shows lack of discipline and organizational skills. Being late is disrespectful to others. It creates a negative reputation and impacts your self-esteem.

If you plan to arrive anywhere on time, it requires preparation. Being on time is passed down in family dynamics just like the habit of being late is passed down. If you were taught at a young age that being a timely person was important, odds are you are seldom late. If being on time has never been a priority in the past for you, it will not be important now. Unless you see a need to change.

There are three types of time categories we can find ourselves in.

1. People who are always on time.

These people are hardworking, disciplined, dependable, organized and of a good reputation. Most of these people are your leaders.

2. People who are on time most of the time.

This is the most dangerous category. People found in this category are the excuse makers. This is a comfort zone for lateness. This is where you will hear sayings like:

"I'm not late all the time."
"I was only late twice last week."
"What's so important about being on time anyway?"

3. People who are never on time.

These people are the ones unorganized, unprofessional, inconsiderate, and just don't give a damn. People who are always late think they are only late sometimes. Success requires that people can depend on you being on time. Being late reveals disrespect or incompetence. No matter how much you think you know about your business, being late will undermine your success.

Chapter 3

How To Be On Time

To start being on time, one must recognize there is a problem. If being late has turned your life into a defining trait of who you are, the underlying causes must be addressed. Being on time may take an attitude adjustment. A lot of times we are late because the event we are showing up for isn't important to us. Don't schedule events that you really don't want to attend.

Getting organized and prioritizing punctuality is a good start.

Here are a few timely tips:

1. Set up the night before.

2. Lay out your clothes.

3. Put your keys, wallet, purse, computer and all other items you must take in a

place easy to locate the next morning.

4. Always *plan* on arriving early.

5. When you have to be somewhere plan to arrive 15-30 minutes before you have to be there.

6. Get up earlier.

7. Set your alarm earlier by the amount of time you are typically late.

8. Get out of bed immediately when the alarm goes off. Don't give yourself any chance to renegotiate yourself to sleep. How many times have 10 minutes turned into 30 minutes? You snooze, you lose.

9. Set your clocks ahead a few minutes if this will help.

10. Remind yourself that being on time is a matter of good manners. Being late is inconsiderate. Being on time is a sign of respect.

11. Get rid of the excuses. *Whatever* your most regular excuse is, stop it.

12. Get the family involved. Make sure everyone in the family knows what their assignment is for the next day.

13. Embrace the wait of getting somewhere early. Read a book, check e-mails, call a friend or family member.

14. Consider the consequences of your being late. Losing that promotion, being docked in your pay, reputation tarnished or losing your job.

15. Be clear on the location you need to go, how to reach it and how long it takes to get there. Check your GPS *before* you get in the car to leave. People are often late because they have a hard time finding the place they are going. They assume they will find the place immediately and are frustrated when that doesn't happen.

16. Trim your schedule. Look at each event on your calendar and evaluate what is a priority. Can you rearrange existing appointments? Sometimes we are late because we pack our schedules too tight May be you can be more aware of your appointments and accept fewer in the future.

17. Watch for time traps like going on-line, video games and watching television. If you have activities that cause you to forget the time, do them when there is space on your schedule.

Conclusion

Recently there has been discussion on the benefits of being late. It's only fair to clear the air about this subject.

In a book titled *Never be Late Again*, the author states "Many people tend to be both optimistic and unrealistic and this affects their perception of time."

People believe they can do a lot of things in one day and they try to do it all. They do this because one time in their lives, maybe years ago, this worked. This could be true but it can lead to being overstretched and disorderly.

At first being on time will to some and can for others, seem strange. You may be the first person at an event. You may get there before the people who are organizing the affair. Don't be discouraged. The payoff is you have become a dependable person. It will not be long before you are proud of your accomplishment of becoming a timely person.

Author Bio

While many people value big houses, fancy cars and positions with lavish titles, he places the greatest value on the one thing none of us can ever get back: *time*. For Richard Hatcher, author and speaker, time doesn't just equal money. It has the power to make or break who you are, what you stand for and what others come to know you as. Having worked with youth for over 30 years, he's not just passionate about seeing them succeed and fulfill their dreams. He's intentional about making sure they get it done *on time*.

Understanding firsthand that if we don't engage the younger generation, we don't have room to complain about their choices, Richard uses a strategic approach to reaching and understanding the hearts of teens. Since his initial work with The Amistad Project, a program for inner city youth in Flint, Michigan, he has been at the ground level supporting youth day to day. And while many only listen to respond, not to hear and understand, he's learned to listen first—and *listen second.* Intentional about building lasting, trusting relationships with young people, he makes it a point to only give advice after building relationship—and then, only if asked.

In addition to studying at Lincoln University in Jefferson City, Missouri, Richard was also honorably discharged from both the U.S Army and Navy. With an intense hunger and thirst for the Word of God, Richard also became a graduate of Word of Life Bible College. As a founding member of The Amistad Project and facilitator for The TeenQuest Program, anyone can see that Richard is not just talking the talk. He's working diligently to leave a lasting impression on his community and generations to come.

Known to many as The Timeologist, Richard's third book, *It's About Time*, encourages readers to know how one handles time can define their brand, business and life in general. For more information or booking, email bernie.hatcher@gmail.com or call 810.394.0139.

Reference List

Statistics:

abcnews.com (March 2007)
Stephn/Flickr (March 11, 2015)
nbcnews.com (April 2016)
careerbuilder.com (January 30, 2017)
Article Titled: At Your Finger Tips
Organizing (January 1, 2018)
sciencealert.com (February 9, 2018)

Stories

Article Titled: Mount Vesuvius and Pompeii - Facts and History
www.LiveScience.com

Article Titled: Communist Party
www.Quora.com
Leung Kwan Pang

Article Titled: Sinking of the R.M.S. Titanic
www.wikipeda.org

Article Titled: Pearl Harbor Memo Shows US Warned of Japanese Attack
www.telegraph.co.uk

Notes:

Notes:

www.ingramcontent.com/pod-product-compliance
Lightning Source LLC
Chambersburg PA
CBHW071804040426
42446CB00012B/2707